LOW VOICE

15 MORE AMERICAN ART SONGS

WITH COMPANION RECORDINGS OF PIANO ACCOMPANIMENTS

Compiled by Richard Walters

T0079131

To access companion recorded accompaniments online, visit:
www.halleonard.com/mylibrary

"Enter Code"
3302-1256-7733-8437

ISBN 978-1-4803-3030-6

G. SCHIRMER, Inc.

DISTRIBUTED BY

Visit Hal Leonard Online at
www.halleonard.com

Contact us:
Hal Leonard
7777 West Bluemound Road
Milwaukee, WI 53213
Email: info@halleonard.com

In Europe, contact:
Hal Leonard Europe Limited
42 Wigmore Street
Marylebone, London, W1U 2RN
Email: info@halleonardeurope.com

In Australia, contact:
Hal Leonard Australia Pty. Ltd.
4 Lentara Court
Cheltenham, Victoria, 3192 Australia
Email: info@halleonard.com.au

CONTENTS

Pianist on the recordings:
LAURA WARD[1]
RICHARD WALTERS[2]

It's all I have to bring

Emily Dickinson*

Ernst Bacon

*Words printed by special permission.

Hey nonny no!

from *Three Songs: The Words from Old England*

Anonymous (16th century)

Samuel Barber

A Slumber Song of the Madonna

Alfred Noyes

Samuel Barber

Here in my arms as I sing thee to sleep! Hush - a - by

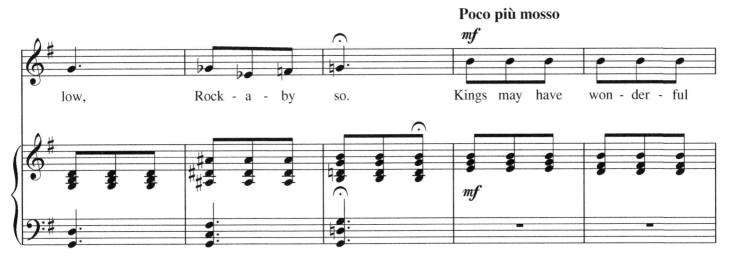

low, Rock - a - by so. Kings may have won - der - ful

Poco più mosso

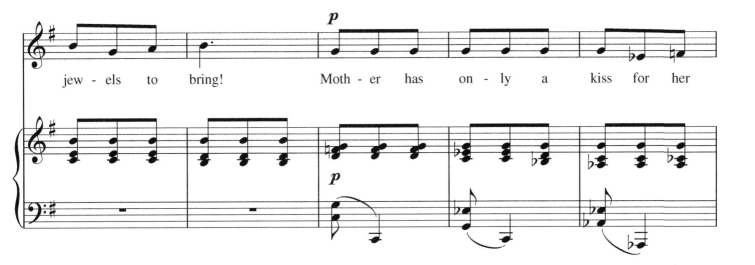

jew - els to bring! Moth - er has on - ly a kiss for her

king. Why should my sing - ing So make me to weep?

On - ly I know that I love thee, I love thee!

Tempo primo

Love thee, my lit - tle one, _____ Sleep!

Mother, I cannot mind my wheel

Walter Savage Landor

Samuel Barber

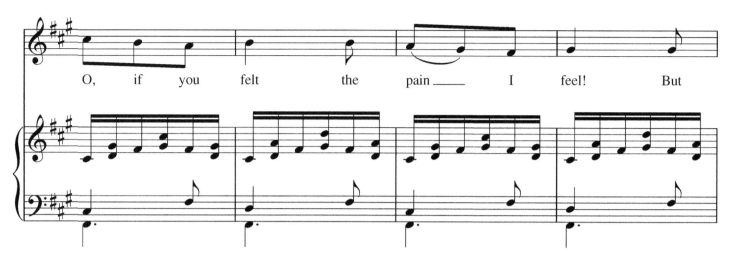

O, if you felt the pain ___ I feel! But

O, ___ who ev - er felt ___ as I? ___

___ No long - er

could I doubt him true— All oth - er

men may use de - ceit; _____ He al - ways said my eyes _____ were blue, And of - ten swore my lips _____ were sweet. _____

The year's at the spring

from *Three Browning Songs,* Op. 44

Robert Browning

Amy Marcy Cheney Beach

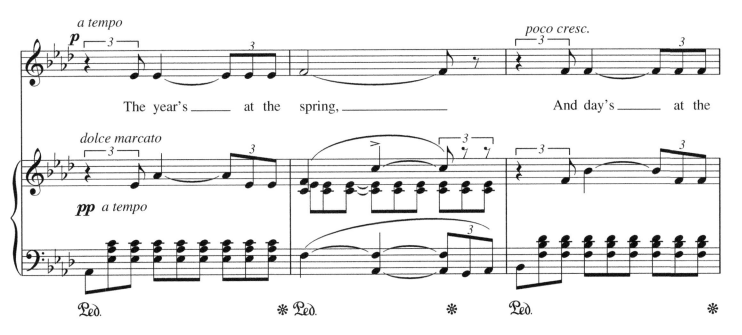

a tempo
p
poco cresc.
The year's at the spring, And day's at the
dolce marcato
pp a tempo
sempre cresc.
morn; The lark's on the wing; The
sempre cresc.
snail's on the thorn; God's in His
f
f

heaven, _____ God's _____ in His heaven, All's _

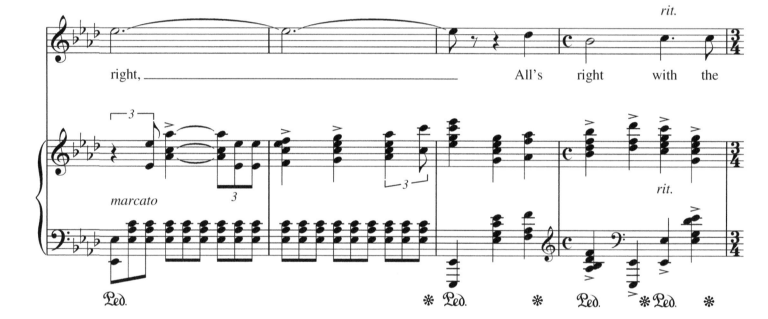

right, _____ All's right with the

world! _____

Where the Music Comes From

Words and Music by
Lee Hoiby

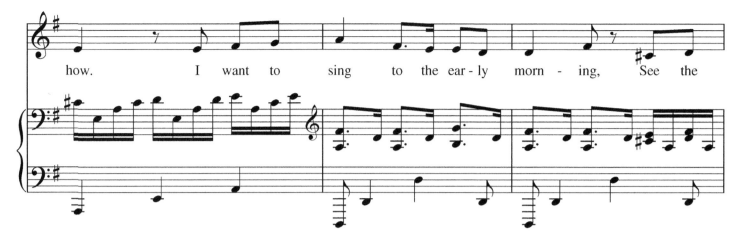

how. I want to sing to the ear - ly morn - ing, See the

sun - light melt the snow; And oh,_____ I want to

grow._____

I want to

wake to the liv-ing spir - it Here in - side me where it lies. I want to

lis - ten till I can hear it, Let it guide me, and re - al - ize That I can

go with the flow un - end - ing, That is blend - ing, that is

real; And oh, _____ I want to

feel.

I want to

walk in the earth-ly gar - den, Far from cit-ies, far from

fear. I want to talk to the grow-ing gar - den, To the

de - vas,* to the deer, And to be one with the riv - er flow - ing, Breez - es blow - ing, sky a - bove; _____ And oh, _____ I want to love. _____

*pronounced *day – vas* (nature spirits)

Sugar in the Cane

Tennessee Williams

Paul Bowles

ba - ker.＿＿ I'm sweet sug - ar in the cane, ＿

Nev - er touched ex - cept by rain.＿＿＿

If you touched me God save you, These sum - mer days are hot and

blue.＿＿＿

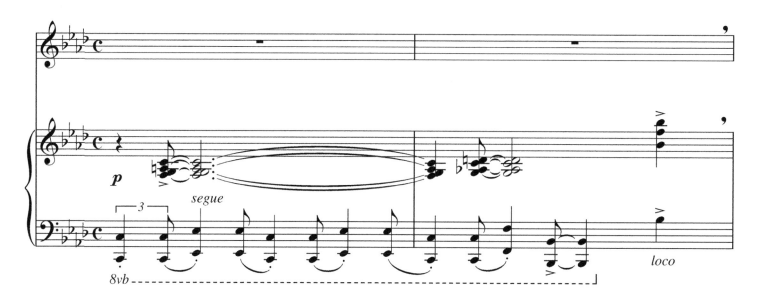

I'm po - ta - toes not yet mashed, I'm a check that ain't been

cashed. _____ I'm a win - dow with a blind, _

Can't see what goes on be - hind. _____

If you did, God save your soul! These win - ter nights are blue and

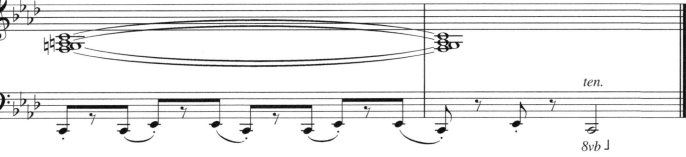

cold! _____

ten.

8vb

February Twilight

Sara Teasdale

John Duke

A sin - gle star _____ looked out From the

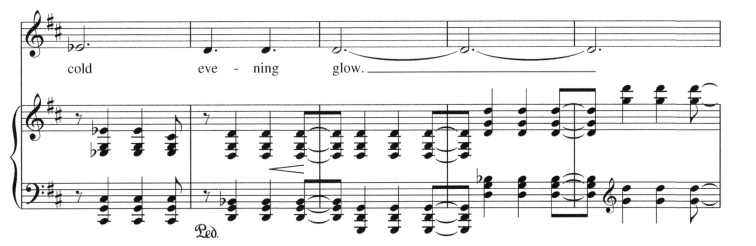

cold eve - ning glow. _____

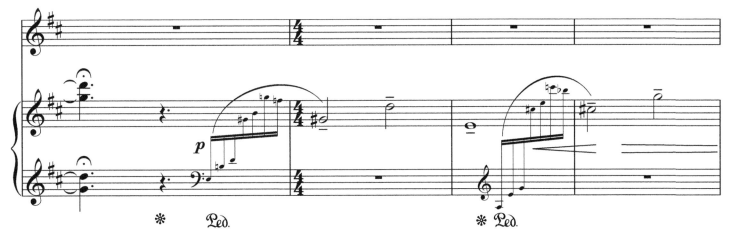

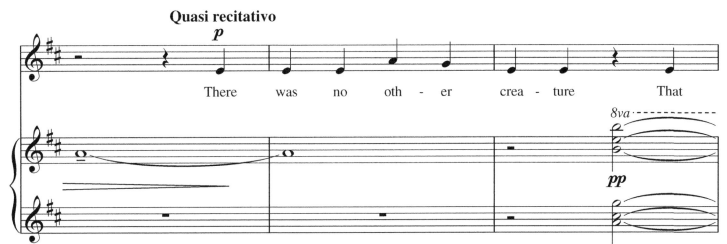

Quasi recitativo

There was no oth - er crea - ture That

saw what I could see; I

stood and watched the eve - ning

star As long as it watched

me.

To Miriam Witkin

The Green Dog

Words and Music by
Herbert Kingsley

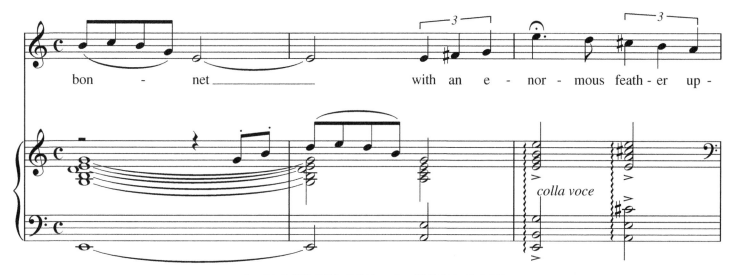

But, a - las! no mat - ter what you've heard, The facts are con - sis - tent - ly ab -

surd, _____ For my dog is - n't green, _____

And, what sets the mat - ter e - ven more a - gog—

I have - n't an - y dog! _____

In the mornin'

Negro spiritual (before 1850) communicated
to Ives in 1929 by Mary Evelyn Stiles

Accompaniment by
Charles Ives

The first chord is played as an introduction on the accompaniment recording.

To Mme. Povla Frijsh

The Pasture

Robert Frost*

Charles Naginski

wait   to watch the   wa - ter clear,_____ I   may):

I   sha'n't be gone   long.—   You   come too.

I'm go-ing out to   fetch   the lit - tle   calf   That's stand-ing   by   the

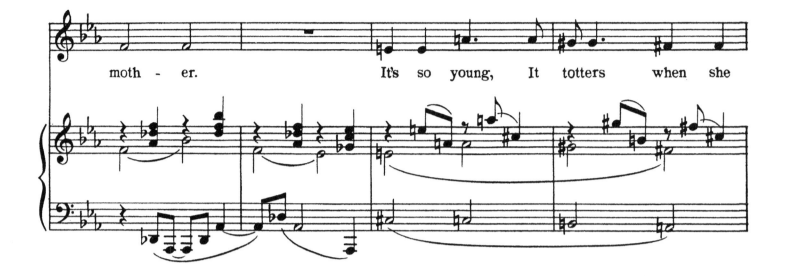

moth - er. It's so young, It totters when she

licks it with her tongue.

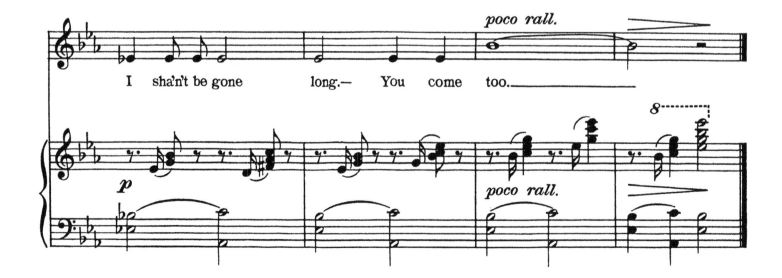

I sha'n't be gone long.— You come too._____

Holiday Song

Genevieve Taggard*

William Schuman
Arranged by the composer

*Words printed by exclusive permission.
**LH 8vb octaves in original key from ** to †

Tempo I moderato ♩ = **circa 100**

When was it ev-er a waste of time to climb ___ hills ___ or to sing on our hills the song of a long jol-ly day in the sun?

Tempo I ♩. **circa 100** *(no slower)*

All of us, ev-'ry-one,

fff with energy and precision

ev-'ry-one, all of us, all of us, ev-'ry-one, ev-'ry-one,

stacc. sempre

**LH 8vb in original key from ** to †

all of us, ev - 'ry-one of us, ev - 'ry-one of us, ev - 'ry-one of us,

ev - 'ry-one of us, all of us, ev - 'ry - one, all of us,

ev - 'ry - one, all of us, ev - 'ry-one of us has

some-thing to sing a - bout, _____ has some-thing to sing a -

bout, to sing and shout, to sing and shout, shout!

8vb

Tempo II circa 160

Lo!   Dee - de - lee dee,   dee - de - lee dee,

Lo!   Dee - de - lee dee,   dee - de - lee dee,   dee - de - lee dee.

p

Dee - a,   dee - a,   dee - a,   dee - a,   Lo! _____

8va

New Rochelle, N.Y.
May 26, 1942
Arranged for solo
voice May, 1946

**LH 8vb in original key from ** to †

Black is the color of my true love's hair

Text collected and adapted by
John Jacob Niles
Music by John Jacob Niles

love___ the grass where - on she stands.

I___ love my_ love and_ well she knows, I

love___ the grass where - on she goes; If___ she on__ earth no__

44

more I see, My life will quick-ly leave me.

I go to Troub-le-some* to mourn, to weep, But

sat - is-fied I ne'er can sleep; I'll write her a note in

a few lit-tle lines, I'll suf - fer death ten thou-sand times.

* Troublesome Creek, which empties into the Kentucky River.

Black, black, black is the col-or of my true love's hair, Her lips are some-thing ro-sy fair, The pert-est face and the dain-ti-est hands— I love the grass where-on she stands.

Go 'way from my window

Words and Music by
John Jacob Niles
Arranged by the composer

both-er me no_ more._ I'll
long as song - birds sing._ I'll
on ac-count of_ you._ Go
real-ly did love best._ Go 'way from my win-dow, Go

'way_ from my door, Go 'way, 'way, 'way from my bed-side And

both-er me no more,_ And both-er me no_ more.

Brother Will, Brother John

Elizabeth Charles Welborn

John Sacco

With sly jocularity ♩ = 82

Voice

Piano

mf

mf

mf

You

can't take it with you, Broth-er Will, Broth-er John, You

can't take it with you, Broth-er Will, Broth-er John, It